Anonymous

The Favorite

Anonymous

The Favorite

ISBN/EAN: 9783744760850

Printed in Europe, USA, Canada, Australia, Japan

Cover: Foto ©ninafisch / pixelio.de

More available books at **www.hansebooks.com**

THE FAVORITE

Uniform with this is published
The Favorite Irish Patriotic Songster, No. 1,
AND
The Favorite Lays of the Green Isle Songster, No. 2.

IRISH SUNBURST SONGSTER.

NEW YORK:
ROB'T M. DE WITT, Publisher,
No. 33 ROSE STREET.

THE FAVORITE

"IRISH SUNBURST"

SONGSTER.

[NO. 3.]

WHAT THE "STARS AND STRIPES" ARE TO AMERICANS—
The " TRI-COLOR " to the FRENCH—the Glorious

' SUNBURST ' IS TO THE · IRISH.

In this TRULY NATIONAL Book of Songs will be seen all those
nobly Patriotic Pieces which kindled enthusiasm in Every
. Irishman's Breast in Exile or in Death ! These Match-
less Songs are pre-eminently fitted for association

THE EMBLEM OF IRISH NATIONALITY.

Uniform with this will be published, No. 1, 'The Favorite Irish
Patriotic Songster,' and No 2. 'The Favorite Let Off the
Green Isle Songster.'

NEW-YORK:

ROBERT M. DE WITT, PUBLISHER,

NO. 33 ROSE STREET,

(Between Duane and Frankfort Streets.)

Entered according to Act of Congress, in the year 1873, by ROBERT
M. DE WITT, in the Office of the Librarian of Congress,
at Washington, D. C.

CONTENTS

OF

THE FAVORITE "IRISH SUNBURST"

SONGSTER.

(No. 3.)

☞ The Music of all the Songs in this book can be obtained at any Music Store in the United States or Canada.

GO, EDMUND, JOIN THE MARTIAL THRONG.

Go Edmund, join the martial throng,
   And nobly seek an honour'd name,
Go pour the tide of war along,
   And climb the rugged steep of fame.
Yet, yet forgive a maiden's fear,
   Whilst valour's toilsome paths you prove
Oh! sometimes wipe the pensive tear.
   And sweetly think of me and love.

On Erin's sod you drew your breath,
   From her you caught the patriot glow,
Whose children spurn the thoughts of death,
   And foremost meet the daring foe;
Yet whilst with pride you scorn to fly,
   Or from the brow of battle move;
Oh! sometimes breathe the tender sigh,
   And dearly think of me and love.

Should Fate your early fall decree,
   Far, far from Erin's parent shore,
Where ne'er my doating eyes might see
   Those looks of manly beauty more;
To heav'n should rise the fervent prayer,
   To meet in lasting bliss above;
Within my breast the wound I'd bear,
   And meekly die for you and love.

Bright sun, before whose glorious ray,
　　Our Pagan fathers bent the knee;
Whose pillar altars yet can say,
　　When time was young our sires were free—
Who seest how fallen their offspring be—
　　Our matrons' tears—our patriot's gore ;
We swear before high Heaven and thee,
　　The Saxon holds us slaves no more !

Our Sunburst on the Roman foe
　　Flash'd vengeance once in foreign field—
On Clontarf's plain lay scathed low
　　What power the Sea-kings fierce could wield
Bein Bnrb might say whose cloven shield
　　'Neath bloody hoofs was trampled o'er ;
And by these memories high, we yield
　　Our limbs to Saxon chains no more !

The *lairseach* wild, whose trembling string
　　Had long the " song of sorrow" spoke,
Shall bid the wild *Rosg-Cata* sing
　　The curse and crime of Saxon yoke.
And, by each heart his bondage broke—
　　Each exile's sigh on distant shore—
Each martyr 'neath the headman's stroke—
　　The Saxon holds us slaves no more !

Send the loud war-cry o'er the main—
　　Your Sunburst to the breezes spread ;
That *slogan* rends the heaven in twain—
　　The earth reels back beneath your tread,
Ye Saxon despots, hear, and dread—
　　Your march o'er patriot hearts is o'er—
That shout hath told—that tramp hath said,
　　Our country's sons are slaves no more !

LAMENT FOR THE DEATH OF EOGHAN
RUADH O'NEIL.

Time—10th Nov., 1649. Scene—Ormond's Camp, County Waterford.
Speakers—a Veteran of Owen O'Neil's clan, and one of the horsemen just arrived with an account of his death.

" Did they dare, did they dare to slay Owen Roe O'Neil !"
" Yes, they slew with poison him they feared to meet with steel."
' May God wither up their hearts! May their blood cease to flow !
May they walk in living death, who poisoned Owen Roe !

Though it break my heart to hear, say again the bitter words."
" From Derry, against Cromwell, he marched to measure swords ;
But the weapon of the Saxon met him on his way,
And he died at Cloc Uactair, upon Saint Leonard's Day."

" Wail, wail ye for The Mighty One ! Wail, wail ye for the Dead ;
Quench the hearth, and hold the breath—with ashes strew the head.
How tenderly we loved him ! How deeply we deplore !
Holy Saviour ! but to think we shall never see him more.

Sagest in the council was he, kindest in the hall,
Sure we never won a battle—'Twas Owen won them all.
Had he lived—had he lived—our dear country had been free ;
But he's dead, but he's dead, and 'tis slaves we'll ever be.

O'Farrell and Clanricarde, Preston and Red Hugh,
Audley and MacMahon—ye are valiant, wise, and true ;
But—what are ye all to our darling who is gone ?
The Rudder of our Ship was he, our Castle's corner-stone !

Wail, wail him through the Island ! Weep, weep for our pride !
Would that on the battle-field our gallant chief had died !
Weep the Victor of Beinn Burb—weep him, young men and old ;
Weep for him, ye women—your Beautiful lies cold !

We thought you would not die—we were sure you would not go,
And leave us in our utmost need to Cromwell's cruel blow—
Sheep without a shepherd, when the snow shuts out the sky :
Oh! why did you leave us, Owen ! Why did you die !

Soft as woman's was your voice, O'Neil ! bright was your eye
Oh : why did you leave us, Owen ! why did you die !
Your troubles are all over, you're at rest with God on high ;
But we're slaves, and we're orphans, Owen ! why did you die !"

THE PRICE OF FREEDOM.

Man of Ireland—heir of sorrow—
    Wronged, insulted, scorned, oppressed—
Wilt thou never see that morrow
    When thy weary heart may rest ?
Lift thine eyes, thou outraged creature ;
    Nay, look up, for *Man* thou art—
Man in form, in frame, and feature—
    Why not act man's godlike part ?

Think, reflect, inquire, examine,
    Is't for this God gave you birth—
With the spectre look of famine,
    Thus to creep along the earth ?
Does this world contain no treasures
    Fit for thee, as Man, to wear ?—
Does this life abound in pleasures,
    And thou askest not to share ?

Look ! the nations are awaking—
    Every chain that bound them burst,
At the crystal fountain slaking
    With parched lips their fever thirst !
Ignorance, the demon, fleeing,
    Leaves unlocked the fount they sip—
Wilt thou not, thou wretched being,
    Stoop and cool thy burning lip ?

History's lessons, if thou'lt read 'em,
    All proclaim this truth to thee ;
Knowledge is the price of freedom—
    Know thyself, and thou art free !

[1]

PRICE FREEDOM.—[Concluded.

Know, oh Man! thy proud vocation—
  Stand erect, with calm, clear brow—
Happy, happy! were our nation
  If thou hadst that knowledge now!

Know thy wretched, sad condition—
  Know the ills that keep thee so—
Knowledge is the sole physician—
  Thou wert healed if thou didst know!
Those who crush, and scorn, and slight thee—
  Those to whom you once would kneel—
Were the foremost then to right thee,
  If thou felt as thou shouldst feel!

Not as beggars lowly bending—
  Not in sighs, and groans, and tears—
But a voice of thunder sending
  Through thy tyrant brother's ears!
Tell him he is not thy master—
  Tell him of man's common lot—
Feel life has but one disaster—
  To be a slave, and know it not!

If thou knew what knowledge giveth—
  If thou knew how blest is he
Who in Freedom's presence liveth,
  Thou wouldst die, or else be free!
Round about he looks in gladness—
  Joys in heaven, and earth, and sea—
Scarcely heaves a sigh of sadness,
  Save in thoughts of such as thee!
[2]

THE UNION

How did they pass the Union?
  By perjury and fraud;
By slaves, who sold for place or gold
  Their country and their God:
By all the savage acts that yet
  Have followed England's track:
The pitchcap and the bayonet,
  The gibbet and the rack
And thus was passed the Union
  By Pitt and Castlereagh:
Could Satan send for such an end
  More worthy tools than they?

How thrive we by the Union?
  Look round your native land!
In ruined trade and wealth decayed
  See slavery's surest brand;
Our glory as a nation gone—
  Our substance drained away—
A wretched province trampled on.
  Is all we've left to-day.
Then curse with me the Union,
  That juggle foul and base,
The baneful root that bore such fruit
  Of ruin and disgrace.

And shall it last, this Union,
  To grind and waste us so?
O er hill and lea, from sea to sea,
  All Ireland thunders, No!
Eight million necks are stiff to bow—
  We know our might as men—
We conquered once before, and now
  We'll conquer once again;
And rend the cursed Union,
  And fling it to the wind—
And Ireland's laws and Ireland's cause,
  Alone our hearts shall bind!

OURSELVES ALONE.

The work that should to-day be wrought
  Defer not till to-morrow;
The help that should within be sought,
  Scorn from without to borrow.
Old maxims these—yet stout and true—
  They speak in trumpet tone;
To do at once what is to do,
  And trust ourselves alone.

Too long our Irish hearts we schooled
  In patient hope to bide;
By dreams of English justice fooled,
  And English tongues that lied·
That hour of weak delusion's past
  The empty dream has flown;
Our hope and strength, we find at last,
  Is in ourselves alone.

Aye! bitter hate, or cold neglect,
  Or lukewarm love at best;
Is all we've found, or can expect,
  We aliens of the west.
No friend beyond her own green shore,
  Can Erin truly own;
Yet stronger is her trust, therefore,
  In her brave sons alone.

Remember when our lot was worse—
  Sunk, trampled to the dust; .
'Twas long our weakness and our curse,
  In stranger aid to trust.
And if at length, we proudly trod
  On bigot laws o'erthrown;
Who won that struggle? Under God,
  Ourselves—ourselves alone.

Oh, let its memory be enshrined
  In Ireland's heart forever;
It proves a banded people's mind
  Must win in just endeavor.
It shows how wicked to despair,
  How weak to idly groan—
If ills at others' hands ye bear,
  The cure is in your own.

The foolish word "impossible."
  At once, for aye disdain;
No power can bar a people's will
  A people's right to gain.
Be bold, united, firmly set,
  Nor flinch in word or tone—
We'll be a glorious nation yet,
  Redeemed—erect—alone.

STANZAS.

By Thomas Furlong.

[Supposed to be written on the night that the Act of Legislative
Union became the law of the land.]

Oh! Ireland, my country—the hour
 Of thy pride and thy splendor hath pass'd;
And the chain that was spurned in the moment of power,
 Hangs heavy around thee at last.
There are marks in the fate of each clime—
 There are turns in the fortunes of men,
But the changes of realms, or the chances of time,
 Can never restore thee again.

Thou art chain'd to the wheel of the foe,
 By links that the world shall not sever,
With thy tyrant, thro' storm and thro' calm thou shalt go,
 And thy sentence is bondage forever.
Thou art doom'd for the thankless to toil,
 Thou art left for the proud to disdain,
And the blood of thy sons, and the wealth of thy soul,
 Shall be wasted and wasted in vain.

Thy riches with taunts shall be taken,
 Thy valor with coldness repaid,
And of millions who see thee thus sunk and forsaken,
 Not one shall stand forth in thine aid,
In the nations thy place is left void,
 Thou art lost in the list of the free,
Even realms, by the plague of the earthquake destroy'd,
 May revive—but no hope is for thee.

THE IRISH MOTHER'S LAMENT.

I'm kneeling by your grave, aroon! the autumn sun shines bright,
Flinging upon the grassy mound a flood of golden light;
The flowers I tended for your sake are drooplng one by one,
While I must weep in hopeless grief above your grave, my son.

The withered leaves are showering down, they cannot break your
  rest;
And fair and bright the gorgeous pall they've flung upon your breast;
I saw them bud and blossom forth, beneath the soft spring sky,
But little dreamed that you, my son, should be the first to die.

I knew that want had paled your cheek, that hunger cast its blight
Upon the crimson lip, and eye, whose very glance was light!
I knew thy powerful arm grew weak, the sweet voice lost its tone;
Yet still watched on, in trembling fear. till death the struggle won.

I longed to yield with cheerfulness the treasure lent to me,
But vainly strove to bow the will, although I bent the knee.
Oh! terrible the inward strife that rends the mother's heart!
They only know who've felt the pang, how hard it is to part,

Was there not plenty in the land! the earth gave forth her store—
The glad and fruitful mother earth, with riches brimming o'er;
Not for the slave who tilled the soil the garnered wealth was won;
Our tyrant masters gorged their fill, and murdered thee, my son!

Were there not stately homes enough, that onr roof-tree must fall,
On the forsaken green hillside I see the blackened wall;
Be calm, my heart, in faith abide, God will not still endure
That tyrant hands shall desecrate the dwellings of the poor.

The dwellings of the virtuous poor, the homes of poverty,
Are sacred in the sight of God, though humble they may be,
Beneath the holy cabin roof the truest prayers may rise,
And many a suffering spirit there, is fashioned for the skies

Mavourneen! hark, the bitter winds are howling round your home.
Sleep on in peace, my own one, sleep, your mother soon will come;
The autumn leaves are showering down upon your place of rest,
And bright and beautiful the pall that wraps your gentle breast.

THE ANTI-IRISH IRISHMAN.

From polar seas to torrid climes,
　Where'er the trace of man is found,
What common feeling marks our kind,
　And sanctifies each spot of ground ?
What virtue in the human heart,
　The finest tribute can command ?
The dearest, purest, holiest best,
　The lasting love of Fatherland.

Then who's the wretch that basely spurns,
　The ties of country, kindred, friends—
That barters every nobler aim,
　For sordid views—for private ends ?
One slave alone on earth you'll find,
　Through Nature's universal span,
So lost to virtue, dead to shame,
　The anti-Irish Irishman.

Our fields are fertile, rich our floods,
　Our mountains bold, majestic, grand,
Our air is balm and every breeze,
　Wings health around our native land,
But who despises all our charms,
　And mocks her gifts where'er he can ?
Who, he, the Norman's sneaking slave,
　The anti-Irish Irishman.

The Norman—spawn of fraud and guile,
　Ambitious sought our peaceful shore,
And leagued with native guilt, despoiled,
　And deluged Erin's fields with gore!
Who gave the foeman footing here ?
　What wretch unholy led her van ?
The prototype of modern slaves,
　An anti-Irish Irishman.

[1]

THE ANTI-IRISH, &c.—[CONCLUDED.

For ages rapine ruled our plains,
  And slaughter raised " his red right hand ;
And virgins shriek'd !—and roof-trees blaz'd—
  And desolation swept the land,
And who would not those ills arrest,
  Or aid the patriotic plan,
To burst his country's galling chains ?
  The anti-Irish Irishman !

Hurrah ! " the sunburst !"—Once again,
  Our oriflamme is on the gale,
With shamrock wreaths encircling,
  The blazon'd glorious words " Repeal !"
The coward slave that quits his post,
  Let Argus eyes the traitor scan,
And infamy eternal brand,
  The anti-Irish Irishman !

KATTY DARLING. (A PARODY)

Och, Katty, my darlin', your rest I'll be breaking,
  For the crow of the ould cock is heard on the hill,
An' the dew from his cape, now the peeler is shakin',
  Yet, Katty my darlin', you're slumbering still.
Och! have ye's forgotten the promise ye's made me,
  Of yer bed and yer board was'nt I to have part,
For a week, for a month, if I liked it forever ;
  Then, dearest, wake up, hear the voice of my heart.

Wake, Katty, my darlin', arise from the floor now,
  And the glim that is out with a lucifer light ;
Och ! where is the bell, that once hung at thy door, now
  Arise in thy beauty and let's in to-night.
Och ! Katty, och ! murder ! the rain is fast fallin',
  To think now, that only a door should us part,
May be you've no ears, so yo'. can't hear me bawlin',
  Oh why are you deaf to the voice of my heart.

[2]

THE WEST'S ASLEEP.

When all beside a vigil keep,
The West's asleep, the West's asleep—
Alas! and well may Erin weep,
When Connacht lies in slumber deep;
There lake and plain smile fair and free,
'Mid rocks—their guardian chivalry—
Sing oh! let man learn liberty
From crashing wind and lashing sea.

That chainless wave and lovely land,
Freedom and Nationhood demand,
Be sure, the great God never plann'd
For slumbering slaves a home so grand.
And, long a brave and haughty race,
Honored and sentinelled the place—
Sing oh! not even their sons' disgrace,
Can quite destroy their glory's trace.

For often in O'Connor's van,
To triumph dash'd each Connacht clan—
And fleet as deer the Normans ran,
Through Coirrsliabh Pass and Ard Rathain.
And later times saw deeds as brave;
And glory guards Clanricarde's grave—
Sing oh! they died their land to save,
At Aughrim's slopes and Shannon's wave.

And if, when all a vigil keep,
The West's asleep, the West's asleep—
A'as! and well may Erin weep,
That Connacht lies in slumber deep.
But—hark!—some voice like thunder spake.
The West's awake, the West's awake!"—
Sing oh! hurrah! let England quake,
We'll watch till death for Erin's sake!

HE SAID THAT HE WAS NOT OUR BROTHER.

He said that he was not our brother—
   The mongrel! he said what he knew—
No, Eric! our dear Island mother,
   He ne'er had his black blood from you?
And what though the milk of your bosom
   Gave vigour and health to his veins —
He *was* but a foul foreign blossom,
   Blown hither to poison our plains!

He said that the sword had enslaved us—
   That still at its point we must kneel,—
The liar!—though often it braved us,
   We cross'd it with hardier steel!
This witness his Richard—our vassal!
   His Essex—whose plumes we trod down!
His Willy—whose peerless sword tassel
   We tarnish'd at Limerick town!

No! falsehood and feud were our evils,
   While force not a fetter could twine—
Come Northmen—come Normans—come Devils!
   We give them our *Sparth* to the chine!
And if, once again he would try us,
   To the music of trumpet and drum,
And no traitor among us or nigh us—
   Let him come, the Brigand! let him come!

THE APPEAL.

Weary and spirit-wore,
Bleeding from every pore,
Wrong casting more and more
Wrecks on her way ;
Rudderless, pilotless, shiftless, in sore distress,
Ireland lies helplessly prostrate to-day.

Struggling for life and air,
Foot sore and bosom bare,
Mourning her hopes so fair,
Faded and gone ;
Painfully, wearily, hard set and drearily,
Grasping at shadows that ever flit on,

Who shall assuage her pain ?
Who shall bid freedom reign ?
Who bring back peace again,
Home to our isle ?   [him,
True souls shall meet him, and strong hearts shall greet
Reflecting the sunrise of liberty's smile.

Who will our purpose aid ?
Where shall our choice be made ?
Where the men not afraid
Erin to free ?
Deceived and deceiving, betrayed when believing,
The bitter fruit bearing of long slavery.

Prophets and Saints of old,
Sires of our Fathers bold,
Rise from your graves so cold,
Waken the few—
The faithful and true men, a host, tho' a few men,
Who'll shield us from danger, and teach us to DO.

Ah. they will defend us,
And rise to befriend us,
Whom kind Heaven sends us,
They never forget
How we kissed the grim halter, for love of the Altar,
And sealed with our lifeblood the bond of their debt.

THE APPEAL.—[CONCLUDED.

Down in the forest glen,
Hiding in savage den,
Fighting the Saxon men,
Years of the past ;
Smiling in sorrow's face, writhing in dark disgrace,
Yielding e'en life itself, true to the last.

Oft on the scaffold high
Rang Erin's dearest cry,
Up to the listening sky,
" *Soggarth Aroon* ;"   [amidst us
The hell-hounds who whipped us, stood awe-struck
That they ere came between us, oh, Erin ma vrone!

Brave were the hearts that bled,
Bitter the tears that shed,
Never from danger fled,
Never from shame ;
And they stinted not measure, of blood or of treasure,
To shelter their Soggarth, and halo his name,

Priests of our Irish land,
Bishops, whom Heaven's hand
Placed in your high command,
Pause well to-day ;
Ruin and vice are rife, save us from bitter strife,
Wolves gather round us, to trample and slay.

Alas, for the poison weeds
Scatter their noxious seeds,
Gladly the serpent feeds
Thoughts such as freeze   [us,
The old feelings that bound us, and treacherously round
Spread doubts of that old love, that grew at your knees.

Ere the dark storm gathers,
O God of our fathers,
Awaken the sleeping, give strength to the brave,
And let Ireland's dark story,
Grow bright in the glory
Of the priesthood who raised her from slavery's grave.

[2]

O'BRIEN THE GOOD.

A patriot's statue! a monument built,
  Not to honor some scion of alien blood ;
Not raised to emblazen the triumph of guilt,
  But graved with the name of O'Brien the Good !

A statue to *him*—the undaunted, the proud,
  The soul whom no bribe could corrupt or allure ;
His form raised aloft o'er the eddying crowd,
  Lis face in the gaze of the rich and the poor.

Oh, place it not there, lest his presence should cast
  A reproach on the tricksters that glide at his feet,
And the hand of the lifeless seem lifted to blast
  The sycophants fawning round tyranny's seat !

Oh, place it not there, lest the light that is fled
  Should glitter an instant again in those eyes,
And a curse seem to fall from the lips of the dead
  On the vileness that revels where liberty dies.

Not there—in the heart of the passer below
  A spark might be lit from the patriot's shrine,
And the charm of his presence enkindle the glow
  That ennobles the slave and makes manhood divine.

Not there—for the lessons men draw from his grave
  Can no longer be taught in the land where he lies—
His name must be barred to the lips of the slave,
  And his monument hid from his countrymen's eyes.

Not there shall they build it ! Some robber who sailed
  'Neath the banner of Britain thrice purpled in blood,
Some cut-throat whom England as victor has hailed—
  Let his be the place of O'Brien the Good.

The princes who scourged us with stripes and with chains,
  And those known alone for their greed and their lust,
May fill each unoccupied site that remains,
  But no spot can be spared to O'Brien the Just.

Yes, hide it away ; in some tenantless lane,
  Some bye-way surrounded by ruins and mud,
Where the stranger, bewildered, may seek it in vain,
  Let the marble be raised to O'Brien the Good.

Yes, hide it away—for the pride of his race,
  Their virtues and zeal were interred with his clay,
And the sight of those features might startle the base,
  And crimson the cheeks of his country to-day.

But hear it, ye false ones, the oath that goes round,
  Ere the hands that have pledged it shall wither to dust
In the land that he loved shall a statue be crowned,
  By the hands of the free to O'Brien the Just.

O'CONNOR'S CURSE.

" And go! (I cried) the combat seek,
Ye hearts that unappalled bore
The anguish of a sister's shriek,
Go '—and return no more!
For sooner guilt the ordeal brand
Shall grasp unhurt, than ye shall hold
The banner with victorious hand,
Beneath a sister's curse unroll'd.
O stranger! by my country's loss!
And by my love! and by the cross!
I swear I never could have spoke
The curse that sever'd nature's yoke,
But that a spirit o'er me stood,
And fired me with the wrathful mood;
And frenzy to my heart was given;
To speak the malison of heaven.

" They would have cross'd themselves, all mute;
They would have pray'd to burst the spell;
But at the stamping of my foot
Each hand down powerless fell!
And go to Athunree!(I cried)
High lift the banner of your pride!
But know that when its sheet unrolls,
The weight of blood is on your souls.
Go where the havoc of your kerne
Shall float as high as mountain fern.
Men shall no more your mansion know;
The nettles on your hearth shall grow,
Dead as the green oblivious flood
That mantles by your walls, shall be
The glory of O'Connor's blood.
Away, away to Athunree.
Where, downward when the sun shall fall,
The raven's wing shall be your pall.
And not a vassal shall unlace
The vizor from your dying face.

" A bolt that overhung our dome
Suspended till my curse was given,
Soon as it pass'd these lips of foam,
Peal'd in the blood-red heaven.
Dire was the look that o'er their backs
The angry parting brothers threw:
But now, behold: like cataracts,
Come down the hills in view
O'Connor's plumed partisans;
Thrice ten Innisfallian clans
Were marching to their doom;
A sudden storm their plumage toss'd,
A flash of lightning o'er them cross'd,
And all again was gloom."

MAN'S MISSION.

Human lives are silent teaching—
　Be they earnest, mild, and true—
Noble deeds are noblest preaching
　From the consecrated few.
Poet-Priests their anthems singing,
Hero swords on corslet ringing,
　When Truth's banner is unfurled
Youthful preachers, genius-gifted,
Pouring forth their souls uplifted,
　Till their preaching stirs the world.

Each must work as God has given
　Hero hand and poet soul—
Work is duty while we live in
　This weird world of sin and dole.
Gentle spirits lowly kneeling,
Lift their white hands up appealing
　To the Throne of Heaven's King—
Strongest natures, cu'minating,
In great actions incarnating
　What another can but sing.

Pure and meek-eyed as an angel,
　We must strive—must agonise ;
We must preach the saint's evangel
　Ere we claim the saintly prize—
Work for a'l—for work is holy—
We fu'fil our mission solely
　When, like Heaven's arch above,
Blend our souls in one emblazon,
And the social diapason
Sounds the perfect chord of love.

[1]

Life is combat, life is striving,
　Such our destiny below—
Like a scythed chariot driving
　Through an onward pressing foe.
Deepest sorrow, scorn and trial
Will but teach us self-denial;
　Like the Alchemists of old,
Pass the ore through cleansing fire.
If our spirits would aspire
　To be God's refined gold.

We are struggling in the morning
　With the spirit of the night,
But we trample on it scorning—
　Lo! the eastern sky is bright.
We must watch. The day is breaking;
Soon like Memnon's statue waking
　With the sunrise into sound,
We shall raise our voice to Heaven,
Chant a hymn for conquest given,
　Seize the palm, nor heed the wound.

We must bend our thought to earnest,
　Would we strike the Idols down;
With a purpose of the sternest
　Take the Cross and wait the Crown.
Sufferings human life can hallow,
Sufferings lead to God's Valhalla—
　Meekly bear, but nobly try,
Like a man with soft tears flowing.
Like a God with conquest glowing,
　So to love, and work, and die!

[2]

A PICTURE OF MUNSTER.

Let the Pilgrim of Beauty roam on as he may,
  From the snows of the north to the regions of wine,
What space can unfold in the light of the day,
  In glories more varied, sweet province, than thine!

Where the sun that at morn scatters fire on the crest
  Of the giant-browed Galtees, rounds southward, and takes
A golden farewell ere he sinks to his nest
  In the arbutus bowers of the legended lakes.

Here grey castles moulder like dreams of the past,
  'Mid the sunshine of morn and the dews of the clime
Here round towers, haunted with shadows, still last
  On the evening inland, like dials of Time.

Streams freshen the meadows by forests of green,
  By moss covered Abbeys, all ruined and bare,
Whose lone chancel casements at twilight are seen
  Like skeleton hands pointed heavenward in prayer.

Here rise the great hills from the pasturing plains—
  Here goldens the cornland by village and lea—
Here rolls the broad Shannon, enriched with the rains,
  By the turrets of Limerick, swift to the sea.

Ah! once by those waters great argosies cast
  From their broad vans at sunset, a heroic gloom:
Ah! once by those mouldering battlements, past
  The dusky browed Spaniard in armour and plume.

The pageant is o'er, but the blood that enshades
  The peasant's rich cheek from that fountain is drawn,
And glows in the dewy-dark eyes of her maids,
  Like the sunned Guadelquiver's first ripple at dawn.

Here feasted the chiefs by the castles broad fire,
  And swelled the wild song of the wandering guest,
'Till the memoried music he struck from his lyre,
  Stirred the sword in the scabbard, the heart in the breast.

Here oft as the battle day gloomed o'er the flood,
  Their fierce cheers gave note of the enemy's flight,
As t ey marched by the turrets of Desmond's wild wood,
  With their reddened spears raised in the evening light.

But lo! while we muse in the light of thy streams,
  That sparkle in fresh diamond dances anigh,
The souls of thy clime, like a splendor in dreams,
  Descend in a radiant train from the sky.

Floats up from the Shannon a shadowy blast,
  Were great Brian's Kincora lies ruined and lone,

A PICTURE OF MUNSTER.—[CONCLUDED.

And a phantom looks down from the clouds of the past,
  And mournfully sighs on the years that are gone·

When discord lay dead as his steel-shining hand
  Waved the terror-struck fleets of the North-men away;
When Peace crowned Victory shone in the land
  Like a warrior's plume on a mid-summer day.

Rude years, but ennobled by battle and toil,
  Proud years, that still rise o'er the ages at rest,
Like turrets that look o'er a fertilized soil,
  As they moulder in mist on the skirt of the west.

And mark, after long barren ages of gloom,
  A new light burns broad on eternity's wing,
And Grattan strides proudly by Liberty's tomb,
  With the tongue of a prophet, the brain of a king:

Great chieftain of Freedom, proud Erin's alone,
  Whose soul like a thunder-cloud born in the blue,
Could shake to its centre, the foreigner's throne,
  While it nurtured the sweet native green with its dew.

Who treads by his side o'er the purple-belled heath,
  With wild scattered hair o'er that forehead so wan,
Whence flashes the upturned eye from its sheath,
  With a glance like the brown-hooded falcon's at dawn!

Ah! rich native Fancy, thy flame never lit
  Such splendors as swarmed from our Curran's bright brain—
Scintillant as spar, to the sparkle of wit,
  Yet soft as the blossom enriched with the rain.

Orphan Isle of the Ocean! how bright is thy sway,
  Though sadly thou sit'st by the western wave,
When the song of thy Moore charms the world on its way,
  When the brain of thy Burke rules the age from his grave.

Ah! when shall thy Genius arise with the power
  To guide thy old storms o'er a fertilised mould,
Pile them high in the west in tranquility's hour,
  And magic their gloom to a glory of gold.

Despair not—though shadowed by memory long.
  Great spirits shall guard thee like planets of flame,
And armored by heaven, prolific and strong,
  With the youth of eternity toil for thy fame;

Yes, nurtured to life by the sun of thy clime,
  New heroes shall pace where thy Glories have trod,
And Voices, yet hushed in the silence of Time,
  Roll up with thine old living echoes to God.

[2]

A NEW YEAR'S SONG.

My countrymen, awake! arise!
  Our work begins anew,
Your mingled voices rend the skies,
  Your hearts are firm and true;
You've bravely marched and nobly met
  Our little green isle through;
But, oh! my friends, there's something yet
  For Irishmen to do!

As long as Erin hears the clink
  Of base ignoble chains—
As long as one detested link
  Of foreign rule remains—
As long as of our rightful debt
  One smallest fraction's due,
So long, my friends, there's something yet
  For Irishmen to do!

Too long we've borne the servile yoke—
  Too long the slavish chain—
Too long in feeble accents spoke,
  And ever spoke in vain—
Our wealth has filled the spoiler's net,
  And gorg'd the Saxon crew;
But oh! my friends, we'll teach them yet
  What Irishmen can do.

The olive branch is in our hands,
  The white flag floats above;
Peace—peace pervades our myriad bands,
  And proud forgiving love!
But, oh, let not our foes forget
  We're *men* as Christians, too,
Prepared to do for Ireland yet
  What Irishmen should do.

There's not a man of all our land
  Our country now can spare,
The strong man with his sinewy hand,
  The weak man with his prayer.
No whining tone of mere regret,
  Young Irish bards, for you;
But let your songs teach Ireland yet
  What Irishmen should do.

And whereso'er that duty lead,
  There—there your post should be,
The coward slave is never freed;
  The brave alone are free.
Oh, Freedom, firmly fixed are set
  Our longing eyes on you;
And though we die for Ireland yet,
  So Irishmen should do.

GREEN PLUMES, TO GREY JACKETS.

By Private MILES O'REILLY.

AIR :—" The Wearing of the Green."

Ring it out from every steeple,
  Call the clans from every fold ;
We're a democratic people,
  And our faith we mean to hold.
We're for mercy to the beaten foe,
  For brothers we have been ;
And what oppression is we know,
  All we who Wear the Green.
    Aye! what oppression is we know,
      All we who Wear the Green—
    In our very bones what it is we know,
      We boys who Wear the Green !

We have felt it in our Sireland,
  With its whip our backs are scored ;
Of the South we'll make no Ireland,
  Scourged with famine and the sword.
'Tis true they tried the rebel game
  But punished they have been ;
And I rather think we've done the same,
  All we who Wear the Green.
    We ourselves have done the very same,
      All we who Wear the Green ;
    And we hope *again* to do the same,
      We boys who Wear the Green !

O. Manhood's proudest duty,
  Is to fight for Manhood's faith ;
And true courage has a beauty,
  That not even crime can scathe.
Into chaos they plunged headward, boys,
  Their guilt we do not screen ;
But our Emmet and Lord Edward, boys,
  Did likewise for the Green !
    Aye! Hugh O'Neil and Owen Roe,
      Were rebels for the Green,—
    Wolfe Tone, and great Lord Edward, boys,
      Did likewise for the Green !

And the day is not far distant
  When our equal boast shall be ;
That our country's crown is glistened
  With our Hancock, Grant and Leo.
By Stonewall Jackson's front of flame,
  And Sherman swift and keen ;
And Meagher, who led on to fame
  Us boys who Wear the Green!
    Tom Meagher, whose brigade of fame
      All wore the plumes of Green,
    And Sheridan, whose deathless name
      Proclaims he Wears the Green !

So " Mercy " be the countersign
  And " Union " the parole ;
While the bugles ring along our line
  And the drums for battle roll.
And the cry shall swell from every mouth
  And on our flags be seen ;
" We're for mercy to the beaten South,
  We beaten of the Green."
    We've a fellow-feeling for the South,
      We Rebels of the Green ;
    For the boys who wore the Grey down South,
      We boys who Wore the Green !

OUR COURSE.

We look'd for guidance to the *blind!*
  We sued for counsel to the *dumb,*
Fling the vain fancy to the wind—
  Their hour is past, and *ours* is come;
They gave, in that propitious hour,
  Nor kindly look, nor gracious tone,
But heaven has not denied us power,
  To do their duty and our own.

And is it true, that tyrants throw
  Their shafts among us, steeped in gall;
And every arrow, swift or slow,
  Points foremost still, ascent or fall—
Still sure to wound us, tho' the aim
  Seem ta'en remotely, or amiss?
And men with spirits feel no shame
  To brook so dark a doom as this.

Alas! the nobles of the land,
  Are like our long-deserted halls,
No living voices, clear and grand,
  Respond when foe or freedom calls;
But ever and anon ascends,
  Low moaning, when the tempest rolls;
A tone, that desolation lends,
  Some crevice of their ruined souls.

So be it—yet shall we prolong,
  Our prayers, when deeds would serve our need;
Or wait for woes, the swift and strong,
  Can ward by strength or 'scape by speed,
The vilest of the vile of earth,
  Were nobler than our proud array,
If, suffering bondage from our birth,
  We will not burst it when we may.

And has the bondage not been borne
  Till all our softer nature fled—
Till tryanny's dark tide had worn,
  Down to the stubborn rock its bed,

[1]

OUR COURSE.—[CONCLUDED.

But if the current cold and deep,
  That channel through all time retain,
At worst, by heaven ! it shall not sweep,
  Unruffled o'er our hearts again.

Up for the land—'tis ours—'tis ours—
  The proud man's sympathies are all.
Like silvery clouds, whose faithless showers,
  Come froz'n to hailstones in their fall.
Our freedom and the sea-bird's food,
  Are hid beneath deep ocean waves,
And who should search and sound the flood,
  If not the sea-birds and the slaves ?

MR. ROONEY'S TRAVELS.

In Ireland so frisky. with sweet girls and whisky,
  We managed to keep care and sorrow aloof;
Our whirling revels made all the blue devils
  Creep out with the smoke through a hole in the roof.
But well I remember, one foggy November,
  My mother cried. Go make your fortune, my lad;
Go bother the ninnies clean out of their guineas,
  Away then I scampered from Ballinatad.

Then to seek for promotion, I walk'd the wide ocean,
  Was shipwreck'd, and murder'd and sold for a slave,
Over mountains and rivers, was pelted to shivers,
  And met on dry land with a watery grave.
But now Mr. Jew-man, has made made me a new-man
  And whisky and Mammora make my heart glad,
To the sweet flowing Liffey I'm off in a jiffey,
  With a wnack for old Ireland, and Ballinafad.

From this cursed station to that blessed nation,
  Again Mr. Rooney shall visit your shore,
Where I'll flourish so gaily my sprig of shillelah ;
  Long life to old Nadab of Great Mogadore,
Oh ! then all my cousins will run out by dozens,
  And out too will hobble old mammy and dad,
At dinner they'll treat us with mealy potatoes,
  And whiskey distill'd at sweet Ballinafad.

[2]

FAG AN BEALACH.

By C. G. DUFFY.

"Hope no more for Fatherland,
  All its ranks are thinned or broken?"
Long a base and coward band
  Recreant words like these have spoken
  But we preach a land awoken;
Fatherland is true and tried
  As your fears are false and hollow
Slaves and Dastards stand aside— :
  Knaves and Traitors, *ı ag an Bealach!*

Know, ye suffering brethren ours,
  Might is strong, but right is stronger;
Saxon wiles or Saxon powers
  Can enslave our land no longer
  Than your own dissensions wrong her.
Be ye one in might and mind—
  Quit the mire where cravens wallow—
And your foes shall flee like wind
  From your fearless *Fag an Bealach!*

Thus the mighty multitude
  Speak in accents hoarse with sorrow—
"We are fallen but unsubdued;
  Show us whence we hope may borrow;
  And we'll figh your fight to-morrow.
Be but cautious, true, and brave,
  Where ye lead us we will follow;
Hill and valley, rock and wave.
  Soon shall hear our *Fag an Bealach!*

Fling our banners to the wind,
  Studded o'er with names of glory;
Worth and wit, and might, and mind,
  Poet young, and Patriot hoary
  Long shall make it shine in story.
Close your ranks—the moment's come—
  NOW, ye men of Ireland, follow;
Friends of Freedom, charge them home—
  Foes of Freedom, *Fag an Bealach!*

BIDE YOUR TIME.

By M. J. BARRY.

Bide your Time—the morn is breaking,
  Bright with Freedom's blessed ray—
Millions from their trance awaking,
  Soon shall stand in firm array.
Man shall fetter man no longer;
  Liberty shall march sublime;
Every moment makes you stronger—
  Firm, unshrinking, Bide your Time!

Bide your Time—one false step taken
  Perils all you yet have done;
Undismayed—erect—unshaken—
  Watch and wait, and all is won.
'Tis not by a rash endeavor,
  Men or States to greatness climb—
Would you win your rights forever?
  Calm and thoughtful—Bide your Time!

Bide your time—your worst transgression
  Were to strike, and strike in vain;
He, whose arm would smite oppression,
  Must not need to smite again!
Danger makes the brave man steady,
  Rashness is the coward's crime,
Be for Freedom's battle ready
  When it comes, but,—Bide your Time!

THE PATRIOT'S BRIDE.

Oh ! give me back that royal dream,
    My fancy wrought,
When I have seen your sunny eyes
    Grow moist with thought ;
And fondly hop'd, dear love, your heart from mine
    Its spell had caught ;
And laid me down to dream that dream divine,
    But true, methought,
Of how my life's long task would be, to make yours bless-
    ed as it ought.

    For your sweet sake,
To watch with you—dear friend, with you !—
    Its wonders break ;
The sparkling Spring in that bright face to see
    Its mirror make—
On summer morns to hear the sweet birds sing
    By linn and lake !
And know your voice, your magic voice, could still a
    grander music wake !

On some old shell strewn rock to sit,
    In Autumn eves,
Where grey Killiney cools the torrid air,
    Hot autumn weaves ;
Or by that Holy Well in mountain lone
    Where faith believes
(Fain would I b'lieve) its secret, darling, wish
    True love achieves,
Yet, oh ! its Saint was not more pure than she to whom
    my fond heart cleaves.

To see the dark mid-winter night
    Pass like a noon,
Sultry with thought from minds that teemed,
    And glowed like June ;
Whereto would pass in sculp'd and pictured train
    Art's magic boon ;
And music thrill with many a haughty strain,
    And dear old tune,
Till hearts grew sad to hear the destined hour to part had
    come so soon.

To wake the old weird world that sleeps,
    In Irish lore ;
The strains sweet foreign Spenser sung,
    By Mulla's shore ;
Dear Curran's airy thoughts, like purple birds,

[1]

THE PATRIOT'S BRIDE.—[Concluded.

That shine and soar;
Tone's fiery hopes, and all the deathless vows,
    That Grattan swore;
The songs that once our own dear Davis sung—ah, me!
    to sing no more.

To search with mother-love the gifts
    Our land can boast—
Soft Erna's isles, Neagh's wooded slopes,
    Clare's iron coast;
Kildare, whose legends gray our bosoms stir
    With fay and ghost;
Gray Mourne, green Antrim, purple Glenmalur—
    Lene's fairy host;
With raids to many a foreign land to learn to love dear
    Ireland most.

And all those proud old victor fields
    We thrill to name;
Whose mem'ries are the stars that light,
    Long nights of shame;
The Cairn, the Dun, the Rath, the Tower, the Keep
    That still proclaim
In chronicles of clay, and stone, how true, how deep
    Was Eire's fame-
Oh! we shall see them all with her, that dear, dear friend
    we two have lov'd the same.

Yet, ah! how truer, tend'rer still
    Methought did seem,
That scene of tranquil joy, that happy home,
    By Dodder's stream;
The morning star, that grew a fixed star,
    With love-lit beam,
The ringing laugh, locked hands, and all the far
    And shining stream
Of daily love, that made our daily life diviner than a dream.

For still to me, dear friend, dear love,
    Or both—dear wife
Your image comes with serious thoughts,
    But tender, rife;
No idle plaything to caress or chide
    In sport or strife,
But my best chosen friend, companion, guide,
    To walk through life,
Link'd hand in hand, two equal, loving friends, true hus-
    band and true wife.

[2]

THE IRISHMAN.

By JAMES ORR.

A United Irishman of 1798, and fought at Antrim.

AIR :—"Vive la."

The savage loves his native shore,
  Though rude the soil and chill the air;
Then well may Erin's sons adore
  Their isle which nature formed so fair.
What flood reflects a shore so sweet
  As Shannon great, or pastoral Bann !
Or who a friend or foe can meet
  So generous as an Irishman !

His hand is rash, his heart is warm,
  But honesty is still his guide;
None more repents a deed of harm,
  And none forgives with nobler pride.
He may be duped, but won't be dared—
  More fit to practise than to plan ;
He dearly earns his poor reward,
  And spends it like an Irishman.

If strange or poor, for you he'll pay,
  And guide to where you safe may be ;
If you're his guest, while e'er you stay,
  His cottage holds a jubilee.
His inmost soul he will unlock,
  And if he may *your* secrets scan.
Your confidence he scorns to mock,
  For faithful is an Irishman.

By honor bound in woe or weal,
  Whate'er she bids, he dares to do;
Try him with bribes,—they won't prevail;
  Prove him in fire—you'll find him true.
He seeks not safety, let his post
  Be where it ought in danger's van;
And if the field of fame be lost,
  It won't be by an Irishman.

Erin ! loved land ! from age to age,
  Be thou more great, more famed, and free;
May peace be thine, or, shouldst thou wage
  Defensive war—cheap victory.
May plenty bloom in every field,
  Which gentle breezes softly fan,
And cheerful smiles serenely gild
  The home of every Irishman !

THE IRISH WIFE.

By T. D. M'Gee.

[In 1376, the statute of Kilkenny forbade English settlers in Ireland to intermarry with the old Irish. James, Earl of Desmond, was the first to violate this law.]

I would not give my Irish wife
   For all the dames of the Saxon land—
I would not give my Irish wife
   For the Queen of France's hand.
For she to me is dearer
   Than castles strong, or lands, or life—
An outlaw—so I'm near her,
   To love till death my Irish wife.

Oh! what would be this home of mine—
   A ruined, hermit-haunted place,
But for the light that nightly shines,
   Upon its walls from Kathleen's face?
What comfort in a mine of gold—
   What pleasure in a royal life,
If the heart within lay dead and cold,
   If I could not wed my Irish wife?

I knew the law forbade the banns—
   I knew my King abhorred her race—
Who never bent before their clans,
   Must bow before their ladies' grace.
Take all my forfeited domain,
   I cannot wage with kinsmen strife—
Take knightly gear, and noble name,
   And I will keep my Irish wife.

My Irish wife has clear blue eyes,
   My heaven by day, my stars by night—
And twinlike truth and fondness lie
   Within her swelling bosom white.
My Irish wife has golden hair—
   Apollo's harp had once such strings—
Apollo's self might pause to hear
   Her bird-like carol when she sings.

I would not give my Irish wife
   For all the dames of the Saxon land—
I would not give my Irish wife
   For the Queen of France's hand.
For she to me is dearer
   Than castles strong, or lands, or life—
In death I would be near her,
   And rise beside my Irish wife!

KATHLEEN BAN ADAIR.

By Francis Davis.

The battle blood of Antrim had not dried on freedom's
    shroud,
And the rosy ray of morning was but struggling thro' the
    cloud;
When, with lightning foot and deathly cheek, and wildly
    waving hair,
O'er grass and dew, scarce breathing, flew young Kath-
leen ban Adair.

Behind, her native Antrim in a reeking ruin lies,
Before her, like a silvery path, Kells's sleeping waters rise;
And many a pointed shrub has pierc'd those feet so white
    and bare.
But, oh! thy heart is deeper rent, young Kathleen ban
Adair.

And Kathleen's heart but one week since was like a har-
    vest morn,
When hope and joy are kneeling round the sheaf of yel-
    low corn;
But where's the bloom then made her cheek so ripe, so
    richly fair,
Thy stricken heart hath fed on it, young Kathleen ban
Adair.

And now she gains a thicket, where the sloe and hazel rise,
But why those shrieking whispers, like a rush of worded
    sighs?
Ah! low and lonely bleeding lies a wounded patriot there,
And every pang of his is thine, young Kathleen ban Adair.

" I see them, oh! I see them, in their fearful red array,
The yoemen, love! the yeomen come—ah! heavens away.
    away!
I know, I know they mean to track my lion to his lair;
Ah! save thy life—ah! save it for thy Kathleen ban Adair.

" May Heaven shield thee, Kathleen!—when my soul has
    gone to rest;
May comfort rear her temple in thy pure and faithful
    breast;
But to fly them, oh! to fly them, like a bleeding hunted
    hare,
No! not to purchase heaven, with my Kathleen ban Adair.

[1]

KATHLEEN BAN ADAIR.—[CONCLUDED.

' I loved, I love thee, Kathleen, in my bosom's warmest
   core—
And Erin, injured Erin, oh! I loved thee even more;
And death, I feared him little when I drove him through
   their square,
Nor now, though eating at my heart, my Kathleen ban
   Adair."

With feeble hand his blade he grasp'd, yet dark with
   spoiler's blood,
And then, as though with dying bound, once more erect
   he stood;
But scarcely had he kiss'd that cheek so pale, so purely
   fair,
When flashed their bayonets round him and his Kathleen
   ban Adair.

Then up arose his trembling, yet his dreaded hero's hand,
And up arose, in struggling sounds, his cheer for mother
   land;
A thrust—a rush—their foremost falls; but ah! good God!
   see there,
Thy lover's quivering at thy feet, young Kathleen ban
   Adair.

But heavens! men, what recked he then your heartless,
   taunts and blows,
When from his lacerated heart ten dripping bayonets rose,
And maiden, thou with frantic hands, what boots it kneel-
   ing there?
The winds heed not thy yellow locks, young Kathleen ban
   Adair.

Oh! what were tears, or shrieks, or swoons but shadows
   of the rest,
When torn was frantic Kathleen from the slaughtered
   hero's breast,
And hardly had his last-heaved sigh grown cold upon the
   air,
When oh! of all but life they robb'd young Kathleen ban
   Adair.

But whither now shall Kathleen fly?—already is she gone,
Thy water, Kells, is tempting fair, and thither speeds she
   on;
A moment on its blooming banks she kneels in hurried
   prayer—
Now in its wave she finds a grave. poor Kathleen ban
   Adair.

[2]

WAKE OF WILLIAM ORR.*

1798.

By DR. DRENNAN.

[Dr. Drennan, the author of this ballad, was one of
the ablest writers among the United Irishmen. His
songs and ballads were chiefly directed to enlist Ulster
in "the Union." His song named "Erin," which fixed
upon Ireland the title of "the Emerald Isle," Moore
esteems among the most perfect of modern songs.]

Here our murdered brother lies;
Wake him not with women's cries;
Mourn the way that manhood ought;
Sit in silent trance of thought.

Write his merits on your mind;
Morals pure and manners kind;
In his head as on a hill,
Virtue plac'd her citadel.

Why cut off in palmy youth?
Truth he spoke, and acted truth.
Countrymen, UNITE, he cried,
And died—for what his Savior died.

God of Peace, and God of Love,
Let it not thy vengeance move,
Let it not thy lightnings draw;
A nation guillotin'd by law.

Hapless nation! rent and torn,
Thou wert early taught to mourn.
Warfare of six hundred years!
Epochs marked with blood and tears!

* Tried and convicted, in October, 1797, for administering the
United Irish oath to a private soldier. Four of the jury made affi-
davits that whisky had been introduced into the jury-room, and
a verdict obtained under the influence of drunkenness and intimi-
dation—notwithstanding which, he was afterwards executed!

[1]

Hunted thro' thy native grounds,
Or flung *reward* to human hounds;
Each one pull'd and tore his share,
Heedless of thy deep despair.

Hapless Nation—hapless Land,
Heap of uncementing sand!
Crumbled by a foreign weight;
And by worse, domestic hate.

God of mercy! God of peace!
Make the mad confusion cease;
O'er the mental chaos move,
Through it SPEAK the light of love.

Monstrous and unhappy sight!
Brothers' blood will not unite;
Holy oil and holy water,
Mix, and fill the world with slaughter.

Who is she with aspect wild?
The widow'd mother with her child;
Child new stirring in the womb!
Husband waiting for the tomb!

Angel of this sacred place,
Calm her soul and whisper peace,
Cord, or axe, or guillotin'
Make the sentence—not the sin.

Here we watch our brother's sleep;
Watch with us, but do not weep;
Watch with us thro' dead of night,
But expect the morning light.

Conquer fortune—persevere!
Lo! it breaks, the morning clear;
The cheerful COCK awakes the skies,
The day is come—arise!—arise!

[2]

GARRYOWEN.

By Dr. R. D. Joyce.

They say a dead man tells no tales,
That silence o'er his tomb prevails,
However blow blind Fortune's gales
     In peace or battle gory.
But we can give that phrase the lie,
For dead men's voices fill the sky,
And float from Limerick's towers on high,
     O'er Garryowen and glory!

O, mighty dead! O, unforgot!
O, heroes of the glorious lot!
Your deeds they sanctify each spot,
     Your names each legend hoary!
From charnel crypts of mouldered bones,
From fosses, walls, and graven stones,
Your voices sound in thunder tones,
     O'er Garryowen in glory!

Thy name, great names, great battles won,
Great deeds by Irish heroes done,
They cry "Unite! Be one! Be one!"
     From ancient graves and gory;
They bid us, brothers, all prepare
For th' hour when we can do and dare,
When Freedom's shout shall rend the air,
     O'er Garryowen in glory!

And we can dare and we can do,
United men and brothers true,
Their gallant footsteps to pursue,
     And change our country's story;
To emulate their high renown,
To strike our false oppressors down,
And stir the old triumphant town,
     With Garryowen in glory!

And when that mighty day comes round
We still shall hear their voices sound—
Our tramp shall roll along the ground
     And shake the mountains hoary.
We'll raise the Sunburst as of yore,
And Limerick's streets and Shannon shore
Shall echo to our shout once more,
     Of Garryowen in glory!

SQUARE-TOED BOOTS.

By T. D. Sullivan.

Air:—" King O'Toole."

Says Johnny Bull to Larcom, "Oh, tell my dear police
To watch those wicked foreigners who much disturb my peace,
Who come across the ocean on no manifest pursuits,
And who swagger down my thoroughfares in square-toed boots.

" Their hats caved in and shapeless, to slight the crown are meant
Their knickerbocks and gaiters show a desperate intent;
Their beards look all seditions, from the tips unto the roots,
But there's mischief beyond measure in their square-toed boots.

" When met by sub-inspectors, high sheriffs, or J. P.'S,
There's something quite defiant in the wag of their goatees;
They never bow submissively; they dream of no salutes,
Save what's hinted in the action of their square-toed boots.

" But now, no more these rovers shall fright me and annoy—
I'll treat them to the beauties of Kilmainham and Mountjoy;
For I've made this resolution, whatever be its fruits,
That my laws shall not be trampled on with square-toed boots."

From Larcom to the Royals the word was sent around,
And fast they seized Americans where'er they could be found;
They dragged them off to prison, and they treated them like brutes,
On a charge of foul conspiracy, and square-toed boots.

But now the news has traveled afar across the sea,
Old Uncle Sam has heard it, and a mighty man is he;
Through all his huge anatomy a thrill of anger shoots,
And like thunder comes the stamping of his square-toed boots.

And Johnny Bull grows fearful, as surely well he may,
When up that giant rises, and strides across his way;
For past experience whispers, what no later fact refutes,
That there's terrible propulsion in his square-toed boots.

SOGGARTH AROON.

Am I the slave they say,
    Soggarth aroon,
Since you did show the way,
    Soggarth aroon,
Their slave no more to be
While they would work with me
Ould Ireland's slavery,
    Soggarth aroon?

Why not her poorest man,
    Soggarth aroon,
Try and do all he can,
    Soggarth aroon,
Her commands to fulfil,
Of his own heart and will,
Side by side with you still,
    Soggarth aroon?

Loyal and brave to you,
    Soggarth aroon,
Yet be no slave to you,
    Soggarth aroon—
Nor, out of fear to you,
Stand up so near to you—
Och! out of fear to you!
    Soggarth aroon.

Who in the winter's night,
    Soggarth aroon,
When the cold blast did bite,
    Soggarth aroon.
Came to my cabin-door,

[1]

And, on my earthen-floor,
Knelt by me sick and poor,
   Soggarth aroon ?

Who on the marriage-day,
   Soggarth aroon,
Made the poor cabin gay,
   Soggarth aroon—
And did both laugh and sing,
Making onr hearts to ring,
At the poor christening,
   Soggarth aroon.

Who as friend only met,
   Soggarth aroon,
Never did flout me yet,
   Soggarth aroon ?
And when my heart was dim
Gave, while his eye did brim,
What I should give to him,
   Soggarth aroon ?

Och ! you, and only you,
   Soggarth aroon !
And for this I was true to you
   Soggarth aroon ;
In love they'll never shake,
When for ould Ireland's sake
We a true part did take,
   Soggarth aroon.

[2]

UNDER THE GREEN FLAG.

By T. D. SULLIVAN.

Come, stand beneath the Green, boys,
  Our ancient Irish Green,
    That would not fade ;
    The truest shade
  The earth has ever seen.
At Mother Erin's call, boys,
  Dear Mother Erin's call,
    Come, let us stand
    With sword in hand
Beside her, one and all.

Fill up those ranks anew, boys,
  Those shattered ranks anew,
    For artful knaves
    And sordid slaves
  Have left them but a few.
But Erin dear has still, boys,
  Our Erin dear has still
    A gallant host
    From coast to coast,
On valley, plain, and hill.

Yes, and beyond them too, boys,
  And far beyond them, too,
    Her pure blood runs
    In loving sons
  Prepared her work to do.
And now, from pole to pole, boys,
  From further pole to pole,
    Some subtle wire
    Conveys the fire
That kindles in her soul.

We'll bid that flame arise, boys,
  That sacred flame arise ;
    The time is near,
    The signs are clear.
  On earth and in the skies.
Whate'er our fate may be, boys,
  Whate'er our fate may be,
    We'll act our parts,
    We'll nerve our hearts,
And die, or set her free.

Then stand beneath the Green, boys,
  Arrayed beneath the Green,
    No flag unfurled
    Through all the world
  Is loved as that has been.
'Twas borne through the past, boys,
  The wild, the stormy past ;
    For every thread
    A hero bled—
'Twill triumph at the last.

THE GREEN AND THE GOLD.

By Dr. R. D. Joyce.

Air:—" Neil McCreaman was a braw Hieland Soldier."

In the soft blooming vales of our country,
  Two colors shine brightest of all,
O'er mountain, and moorland, and meadow,
  On cottage and old castle wall;
They shine in the gay summer garden,
  And glint in the depths of the wold,
And they gleam on the banner of Ireland.
  Our colors! the Green and the Gold!
    Then hurrah, for the Green and the Gold!
    By the fresh winds of Freedom out-rolled,
  As they shine on the brave Irish banner,
    Our colors! the Green and the Gold!

In the days of Fomorian and Fenian,
  These colors flashed bright in the ray;
And their gleam kept the fierce Roman eagles
  In Rome conquered Britain at bay,
When Conn forgot his hundred red battles,
  And the lightning struck Daithi of old,
As he bore through Helvetia's wild gorges
  Our colors! the Green and the Gold!
    Then hurrah, for the Green and the Gold!
    May they flourish for ages untold,
  May they blaze in the vanguard of freedom,
    Our colors! the Green and the Gold!

Up many a grim breach of glory,
  In many a fierce battle's tide,
Flashing high o'er the red gleaming surges,
  Our banners swept on in their pride.
From the day when triumphant they fluttered
  O'er the legions of Brian the Bold;
Till with Sarsfield they streamed down the Shannon,
  Our colors! the Green and the Gold!
    Then hurrah, for the Green and the Gold!
    In victory's van as of old
  May they flash over new Fenian legions,
    Our colors! the Green and the Gold!

In these dark days of doom and disaster,
  Is it dead the old love for our land?
Are our bosoms less brave than our fathers',
  Comes the sword-hilt less deft to our hand?
No, we've proved us the wide world over
  Wherever war's surges have rolled,
And will raise once again in Old Ireland,
  Our colors! the Green and the Gold!
    Then hurrah for the Green and the Gold!
    And hurrah for the valliant and bold
  Who will raise them supreme in old Ireland,
    Our colors! the Green and the Gold!

THE BARDS.

Oh, for the Bards, the glorious Bards, the pride of the
    days of old,
When the honour'd claim of   manly name was not found-
    ed on the servile gold;
When the chiefs of our land with chivalrous hand gave
    Genius a regal crown,
While the soulless knave to a nameless grave like a grove-
    ling worm went down.
        When with godlike might
        Worth, fame, and right
        Were defended by steel-nerved men;
        O God of the Free,
        It was grand to see
        The pomp of our country then.

Here's to the Bards, the brave old Bards, who kindled the
    martial fire,
In Chief and Prince with the eloquence and magic of
    harp and lyre;
When the soul of the proud like a lightning cloud flamed
    up at the thrill of song,
And leapt to the fight with a fierce delight to avenge an
    unmanly wrong.
        For the brave Bards gave,
        Like a mountain wave,
        A sweep to the warrior's brand,
        And fired him to show,
        The mark of his blow,
        When a tyrant was in the land.

The Norman Lords, with their valorous swords to our Isle
    as Invaders came,
But soon they grew to that land more true than the Irish
    in birth and name;
For our Island song, with a witchery strong on their
    souls threw an Irish spell,
And their brave hearts felt the fire of the Celt, and they
    show'd they lov'd Erin well.

[1]

THE BARDS, &c.—[Concluded.

But gone are the Bards,
And the warrior lords,
The pride of the times of yore;
And a bloodless race
Has taken their place,
Where fremen are seen no more.

O! splendid days when love and praise were the meed of
the bold and true—
When hands were strong to resent a wrong, and traitors
and knaves were few;
When no hireling spy dared come to pry round the homes
of the toiling poor,
For our Princes ruled with a rod of gold, in their
people's love secure.
And the halls of the peer,
Shook with roaring cheer,
And the traveller was welcomed in!
O God of the brave!
It was grand to live,
In the Kingdom of Erin then.

Then here's to the Bards, the proud old Bards, that hurled
our clans to fight,
Like the headlong dash of a thunder-crash, 'gainst a
foreign invaders might;
When our chieftains broke from Henry's yoke, what
sharpen'd their battle swords,
To strike for their right with courage and might?—'twas
the songs of our brave old Bards.
High souls of song!
Stern foes of wrong,
Since perished our order grand,
The lions are dead,
The eagles have fled,
And jackals have curst the land.
[2]

THE PETTICOAT.

By Dr. R. D. Joyce.

Air:—"I am a roving Doctor."

Since the days of Trojan Paris
  When beauteous Helen was the toast,
O'er lords and mighty monarchs
  The women they have ruled the roast.
And why should croppies hang behind
  In gallantry such men of note?
On Irish ground, in Irish wind
  We spread our flag—a Petticoat!
    For we were croppy heroes
      With pike in hand, and flag afloat,
    Who fought and bled for freedom
      Beneath that flag—the Petticoat!

This Petticoat was broidered
  By fingers fair as fair could be,
And once its folds fell over
  A gleaming ancle gracefully.
A milk-white foot that stept the glades
  As light as fairies of the moat,—
Young Nora's, pride of Wexford maids,
  This tyrant-conquering Petticoat!
    And we were croppy heroes
      With pike in hand, and flag afloat,
    With stains of blood upon it—
      This flag—the conquering Petticoat!

'Twas on a summer morning
  As we marched down the dewy hill,
We found our bright-eyed Nora
  Upon the way-side stark and still.
A yeoman's bullet in her breast,
  A sabre wound across her throat—
'Twas then we made with vengeful zest
  Our banner of her Petticoat!
    For we were croppy heroes
      With pike in hand, and flag afloat,
    Determined to avenge her
      Beneath that flag—the Petticoat!

[1]

THE PETTICOAT.—[CONCLUDED.

The blood spots scarce were faded,
　Ere we their crimson did renew ;
Upon the hill of Oulart
　Her murderers, every man, we slew.
From field to field, from town to town,
　In England's reddest blood we wrote
The story of that Kirtle Gown,
　　The blood-stained, conquering Petticoat !
　　　For we were croppy heroes
　　　　With pike in hand, and flag afloat—
　　　The terror of our tyrants
　　　　Beneath that flag—the Petticoat !

And if great lords and monarchs
　Are so polite to womankind,
The world for our devotion
　To Nora's skirts, no fault can find—
If England's king her life could take,
　Could condescend to cut her throat,*
Brave boys, it was no shame to make
　Our banner of her Petticoat !
　　　For we were croppy heroes
　　　　With pike in hand, and flag afloat,
　　　And bravely we avenged her
　　　　Beneath that flag—the Petticoat !

Then all you roving heroes
　Attend to Theig, the croppy's song ;
May God preserve Old Ireland,
　And Fenian rule therein prolong !
May tyrants there who spoil the land
　All sink in black perdition's boat,
And may it rise to great command,
　The influence of the Petticoat !
　　　And we were croppy heroes
　　　　With pike in hand, and flag afloat,
　　　Who taught our blood-stained tyrants
　　　　The Lesson of the Petticoat !

* The warlike old croppy means that the King cut her throat by
deputy, which was all the same to poor Nora. Theig, the croppy's relation will be received, I suppose only as tradition, but
the petticoat banner is mentioned in the histories of the period.

SONG OF THE GALLOPING O'HOGAN.*

By Dr. R. D. Joyce.

Air:—" He thought of the charmer, &c.'

Hurrah ! boys, hurrah ! for the sword by my side,
The spur and the gallop o'er bogs deep and wide ;
Hurrah ! for the helmet and shining steel jack,
The sight of the spoil, an' good men at my back !
 An' we'll sack and burn for King and sireland,
 An' chase the black foe from ould Ireland !

At the wave of my sword start a thousand good men,
And we ride like the blast over moorland and glen ;
Like dead leaves of winter in ruin an' wrath,
We sweep the cowed Saxon away from our path.
 An' we'll sack and burn for King and sireland,
 An' chase the black foe from ould Ireland !

The herds of the foe graze at noon by the rills,
We have them at night in our camp 'mid the hills ;
Their towns lie in peace at eve of the night,
But they're sacked an' in flames ere the next morning
  light !
 An' we'll sack and burn for King and sireland,
 An' chase the black foe from ould Ireland !

And so we go ridin' by night and by day,
An' fight for our country an' all the rich prey ;
The roar of the battle, sweet music we feel,
An' the light of our hearts is the flashin' of steel !
 An' we'll sack and burn for King and sireland,
 An' chase the black foe from ould Ireland !

*One of the Rapparee chiefs in the time of King James the Second.

THE YOUNG ENTHUSIAST.

By Thomas Francis Meagher.

Though young that heart, though free each thought,
   Though free and wild each feeling,
And though with fire each dream be fraught
   Across those bright eyes stealing—

That heart is true, those thoughts are bold ;
   And bold each feeling sweepeth.
There lies not there a bosom cold,
   A pulse that faintly sleepeth.

His dreams are idiot-dreams, ye say,
   The dreams of fairy story ;
Those dreams will burn in might one day
   And flood his path with glory !

Thou old dull vassal ! fling thy sneer
   Upon that young heart coldly,
And laugh at deeds *thy* heart may fear,
   Yet *he* will venture boldly.

Ay. fling thy sneer, while dull and slow
   Thy withered blood is creeping ;
That heart will beat, that spirit glow,
   When thy tame pulse is sleeping.

Ay, laugh, when o'er his country's ills
   With manly eye he weepeth ;
Laugh, when his brave heart thorbs and thrills,
   And thy cold bosom sleepeth.

Laugh when he vows in heaven's sight,
   Ne'er to flinch—ne'er to falter ;
To toil and fight for a nation's right.
   And guard old Freedom's altar.

Ay, laugh when on the fiery wing
   Of hero thought ascending,
To fame's bold cliff, with eagle spring
   That young bright mind is tending.

He'll gain that cliff, he'll reach that throne,
   The throne where genius shineth,
When round and through thy nameless stone,
   The green weed thickly twineth.

BOOKER'S RUN.

By T. D. SULLIVAN.

AIR :—" The King of the Cannibal Islands."

Oh, list and hear, good friends, from me,
The news that's just come o'er the sea,
About the light-legged company
   Led on by Colonel Booker,
The "Queen's Own Regiment" was their name.
From fair Toronto town they came,
To put the Irish all to shame,
And win themselves immortal fame,
   Tantora, rubadub, oh, hi-ho !
   Drums beat up and bugles blow,
   Off they march to meet the foe,
The Queen's and Colonel Booker,

Such fury filled each loyal mind,
No Volunteer would stay behind ;
They flung their red flag to the wind.
   " Hurra, my boys," said Booker.
"Behold, beyond yon sloping heights,
Their bayonets flashing in the light ;
Go forth, my heroes, left and right,
Let none among them live to night—
   Readily, steadily, oh, hi-ho,
   Sure your aim, and strong your blow,
   No Irish ruck could face, you know,
The Queen's and Colonel Booker."

The rifles flashed, the balls came by,
The Queen's men fell with groan and cry—
"Good Lord, I'd give the world that I
   Were safe at home," said Booker.
He spurred for shelter here and there,
He wheeled and cantered to the rear,

[1]

BOOKER'S RUN. [CONCLUDED.

'While every loyal Volunteer
Was shaking in his boots with fear.
  Quailing, failing, oh, hi-ho,
  Afraid to face the Irish foe,
  Who cheered and laughed to see the show,
The Queen's and Colonel Booker.

" What sound is that comes o'er the breeze ?
Are those their horsemen midst the trees ?
Down, soldiers, down upon your knees
  To meet their charge," said Booker.
Then turning quick, he left the place,
He wished, he said, to "change his base ;"
His soldiers joined him in the race,
And all went off at railroad pace ;
  Helter-skelter, oh, hi-ho,
  Higgledly, piggledy, there they go,
  Swords and guns away they throw,
The Queen's and Colonel Booker.

Oh, never say the Indian breed
Bear off the palm for wind and speed ;
What dusky chief could take a lead
  From loyal Colonel Booker ?
Bid him bring out, by day or night,
His gallant " Queen's " equipped for fight,
Place Colonel John O'Neill in sight
Amidst a ridge of bayonets bright—
  Then give the word, and oh, hi-ho,
  See how they'll fly the Irish foe,
  See how they'll ply the heel and toe,
The Queen's and Colonel Booker.

[2]

THE PEOPLE.

By Dr. R. D. Joyce.

Air:—" All the way to Galway."

A little bird sang in mine ear
With voice prophetic, sweet and clear,—
"Bright Freedom's happy day is near
　For Ireland and her People?"
　　The People! The People!
　　God bless the Irish People!
　　Through all their years
　　Of blood and tears,
　Old Ireland's gallant People!

With gibbet, fire and fetter girth,
With bloody wars and famine dearth,
Our tyrants strove from off the earth
　To blot old Ireland's People!
　　The People! The People!
　　But firm as Shandon steeple
　　Upon its rock,
　　They stood each shock
　Old Ireland's gallant People!

For as the oak tree by the glen
Shorn by the axe, springs up again
From deepest roots beyond our ken,
　So flourished Ireland's People!
　　The People! The People!
　　Though wars cut down the People
　　Each springing root
　　Bore tenfold fruit,—
　Old Ireland's gallant People!

Then, brothers, here's to our dear land!
With freemen may her shores be manned!
And down with England's gory hand!
　And up with Ireland's People!
　　The People! The People!
　　Like bells from Shandon steeple,
　　With ringing chime
　　Sing out sublime
　Hurrah! for Ireland's People!

WHY WE WEAR THE GREEN.

By J. A. JOYCE.

AIR:—" Wearing of the Green."

When God raised up our Island,
  'Mid the billows of the West;
And with vale, and stream, and highland,
  Made beautiful her breast.
The smiling sun flung round her
  A robe of golden sheen;
And the misty west wind crown'd her
  With a garland over Green.

Soon the Gaelic warrior galleys
  Sailed to the shining shore;
And brave men and beauteous women
  Came to dwell forever more.
And their sacrificial fires
  On their altars high were seen;
When the sun and winds they worshipped
  For their glorious gift of Green.

But the Pagan fires faded,
  And the Druid altars fell;
When Patrick came, with glowing words,
  His nobler truths to tell.
" In the Shamrock, lo! the emblem
  Of the Trinity is seen "—
'Twas thus he consecrated here
  The Wearing of the Green.

And the nation's heart leaped to it,
  And thence for evermore;
On their breasts and in their banners,
  The flashing tint they bore.
On their breasts and in their banners
  The gleaming hue was seen;
And the proudest foes went down before
  The men who bore the Green.

So we wear it, and *will* wear it,
  In memory of the brave—
The true and tried, who strove and died
  Our nation's rights to save!
Of those who nobly cherished it,
  When smote oppression keen;
Of those who pine in prison
  For the love they bear the Green.

A PROSPECT.

By EDWARD LYSAGHT.

[Edward Lysaght was born in Brickhill, County Clare. He entered Trinity College in 17.9, and was subsequently called to the Bar. He was generally known as "pleasant Ned Lysaght," and, to use the words of Sir Jonah Barrington, " considered *law* as his *trade*. and conviviality his profession." He wrote some good national songs, which, owing to his having obtained a government p'ace, were omitted from his published collection. The following song was written against the Union]

How justly alarmed is each Dublin cit,

   That he'll soon be transformed to a clown, sir,

By a magical move of that conjurer, Pitt,

   The country is coming to town, sir !

CHORUS.

   Give Pitt, and Dundas, and Jenky a glass,

     Who'd ride on John Bull, and make Paddy an Ass,

Thro' Capel street soon as you'll rurally range,

   You'll scarce recognize it the same street ;

Choice turnips shall grow in your Royal Exchange,

   Fine cabbages down along Dame street.

                Give Pitt, &c.

Wild oats in the College won't want to be till'd ;

   And hemp in the Four Courts may thrive, sir !

[1]

A PROSPECT.—[Concluded.

Your markets again shall with muttons be fill'd—
  By St. Patrick, they'll graze there alive, sir!
                  Give Pitt, &c.

In the Parliament House, quite alive, shall there be
  All the vermin the island e'er gathers;
Full of rooks, as before, Daly's club-house you'll see,
  But the pigeons won't have any feathers.
                  Give Pitt, &c.

Our Custom-house quay, full of weeds, oh, rare sport,
  But the ministers' minions, kind elves. sir!
Will give us free leave all our goods to export,
  When we've got none at home for ourselves, sir!
                  Give Pitt, &c.

Says an alderman—" Corn will grow in your shops;
  This Union must work your enslavement."
"That's true," says the sheriff, " for plenty of *crops**
  Already I've seen on the pavement."
                  Give Pitt, &c.

Ye brave loyal yeoman, dressed gaily in red,
  This minister's plan must elate us;
And well may John Bull, when he's robb'd us of bread,
  Call poor Ireland " *The land of Potatoes.*"
                  Give Pitt, &c.

*A term used for the rebels in 1798, who wore their hair cut close.

[2]

SONG FROM THE BACKWOODS.

Deep in Canadian woods we've met,
 From one bright island flown;
Great is the land we tread, but yet
 Our hearts are with our own.
And ere we leave this shanty small,
 While fades the autumn day,
  We'll toast old Ireland!
  Dear old Ireland!
  Ireland, boys, hurrah!

We've heard her faults a hundred times
 The new ones and the old,
In songs and sermons, rants and rhymes,
 Enlarged some fifty fold.
But take them all, the great and small,
 And this we've got to say:—
  Here's dear old Ireland!
  Good old Ireland!
  Ireland, boys, hurrah!

We know that brave and good men tried
 To snap her rusty chai ,
That patriots suffered, martyrs died,
 And all, 'tis said, in vain;
But no, boys, no! a glance will show
 How far they've won their way—
  Here's good old Ireland!
  Loved old Ireland!
  Ireland, boys, hurrah!

We've seen the wedding and the wake,
 The patron and the fair;
The stuff they take, the fun they make,
 And the heads they break down there.

[1]

With a loud " hurroo" and a " pillalu,"
  And a thundering "clear the way!"—
    Here's gay old Ireland!
    Dear old Ireland!
    Ireland, boys, hurrah!

And well we know in the cool grey eves,
  When the hard day's work is o'er,
How soft and sweet are the words that greet
  The friends who meet once more;
With " Mary machree! and " My Pat! 'tis he!"
  And "My own heart night and day!"
    Ah, fond old Ireland!
    Dear old Ireland!
    Ireland, boys, hurrah!

And happy and bright are the groups that pass
  From their peaceful homes, for miles
O'er fields, and roads, and hills, to Mass,
  When Sunday morning smiles!
And deep the zeal their true hearts feel
  When low they kneel and pray.
    Oh, dear old Ireland!
    Blest old Ireland!
    Ireland, boys, hurrah!

But deep in Canadian woods we've met,
  And we never may see again
The dear old isle where our hearts are set,
  And our first fond hopes remain!
But come, fill up another cup,
  And with every sup let's say—
    Here's loved old Ireland!
    Good old Ireland!
    Ireland, boys, hurrah!

[2]

OLD SKIBBEREEN.

By Patrick Carpenter.

Air:—'The wearing of tho Green."

Young America and his Irish Father.

"O! father, dear, I've often heard you speak of Erin's Isle—
Its scenes how bright and beautiful, how "rich and rare"
   they smile;
You say it is a lovely land in which a Prince might dwell,
Then why did you abandon it, the reason to me tell?"

" My Son, I've loved my native land with fervor and with
   pride—
Her peaceful groves, her mountains rude, her valleys green
   and wide,
And there I've roamed in manhood's prime, and sported
   when a boy,
My Shamrock and shillelagh sure my constant boast and
   joy.

" But lo! a blight came o'er my crops, my sheep and
   cattle died,
The rack-rent too, alas! was due, I could not have supplied;
The landlord drove me from the cot where born I had
   been,
And that, my boy's the reason why I left old *Skibbereen.*

" O! what a dreadful sight it was that dark November
   day;
The Sheriff and the Peelers came to send us all away;

[1]

They set the roof a-blazing with a demon smile of spleen,
And when it fell, the crash was heard all over Skibbereen.

"Your Mother dear, God rest her, fell upon the snowy
   ground,
She fainted in her anguish at the desolation round ;—
She never rose, but passed away from life's tumultuous
   scene,
And found a quiet grave to rest in poor old Skibbereen.

" Ah ! sadly I recall that year of gloomy '48 ;
I rose in vengeance with "the boys" to battle against fate ;
We were hunted thro' the mountains wild, as traitors to
   the Queen,—
And that, my boy's the reason why I left old Skibbereen.

" You then were only two years old, and feeble was your
   frame,
I would not leave you with my friends—you bore my
   father's name !—
I wrapped you in my " *Catamore*" at dead of night unseen,
Then heav'd a sigh, and bade good-by to poor old Skibbereen."

" O ! Father, Father, when the day for vengeance we will
   call,—
When Irishmen o'er field and fen shall rally one and all,—
I'll be the man to lead the van beneath the flag of green,
While loud on high we'll raise the cry—Revenge for
   Skibbereen !"

[2]

ERIN'S PATRIOT GIRLS.

It cheers an Irish exile's heart
    Above all other joys;
To act an unpretending part
    With comrade Irish Boys.
And as we prize that sister link,
    Of lovely, living pearls;
Right gallantly we rise to drink
    Green Erin's Patriot Girls!

Though thoughtless flirts and dainty dames
    Of Irish birth or blood,
Look coldly on the hopes and aims
    Of our dear sisterhood.
We'll have their sympathy to cheer
    The " wild geese " through all perils—
Still you are doubly near and dear,
    Green Erin's Patriot Girl's!

Our Celtic mothers hurled the stones
    From Limerick's granite walls.
And changed the wassail shout to moans
    In Norman robber halls!
They scorned to wed their father's foes,
    Or smile on *shoneen** carls;
And such is still the faith of those—
    Green Erin's Patriot Girls.

Our last great struggle for the cause,
    In glorious Ninety-eight;
Had woman's tearful, sweet applause,
    The pikes to stimulate.
And *grissets* glowed, and bullets grew
    As fast as flax-wheel whirls;
The work you're longing now to do,
    Green Erin's Patriot Girls!

With hopeful hearts we pledge once more
    Our gentle sister guests!
We drew our love of Gaelic lore
    From Irish mothers' breasts.
Then, comrades, let us proudly toast
    These priceless Celtic pearls—
Real shamrock buds, the exile's toast,
    Green Erin's Patriot Girls!

—A Celtic word of ridicule, meaning " upstart."

www.ingramcontent.com/pod-product-compliance
Lightning Source LLC
Chambersburg PA
CBHW021530090426
42739CB00007B/872